THIS CANDLEWICK BOOK BELONGS TO:

_____

_____

_____

For my dear friend, Phyllis Dolgin
D. R.

Thank you, God.
This book is dedicated to the memory of
Pastor Thurman Mitchell. And it is for all of those enslaved
whose suffering was never known or has been forgotten.
S. W. E.

Text copyright © 2002 by Doreen Rappaport
Illustrations copyright © 2002 by Shane W. Evans

First paperback edition 2006

The Library of Congress has cataloged the hardcover edition as follows:
Rappaport, Doreen.
No more! : stories and songs of slave resistance / Doreen Rappaport ;
illustrated by Shane W. Evans. — 1st ed.
p.   cm.
ISBN 978-0-7636-0984-6 (hardcover)
1. Slavery — Juvenile literature. [1. Slavery.] I. Evans, Shane W., ill. II. Title.
HT871 .R36 2002
306.3'62—dc21 00-029756

ISBN 978-0-7636-2876-5 (paperback)

10 11 12 13 14 15 SCP 10 9 8 7 6 5 4 3 2
Printed in Humen, Dongguan, China

This book was typeset in Integrity.
The illustrations were done in oil.

Candlewick Press
99 Dover Street
Somerville, Massachusetts 02144

visit us at www.candlewick.com

No More!

STORIES AND SONGS OF
SLAVE RESISTANCE

Doreen Rappaport

illustrated by Shane W. Evans

CANDLEWICK PRESS

About This Book

I grew up in a house filled with music. My father was a vocal arranger; my mother was a singer. My father marveled at how human beings had used their own musical instrument—the voice—throughout history to express their feelings and tell about their lives. He was fascinated by music of all cultures—especially Negro spirituals, as they were called in those days. He loved the inventiveness and blending of musical elements from the African tradition with those of the Euro-American experience; he treasured the unique music created by the enslaved Africans. He was grateful to James Weldon Johnson, J. Rosamond Johnson, Carl Sandburg, and Alan Lomax, who had traveled the United States, listening, collecting, and notating this great body of music to make it available to all Americans. We listened to this music together and I began to understand how it fortified, insulated, and unified African Americans from the oppressive white world around them.

Then, twenty years ago, I discovered a most amazing poem, "My Pa Was Never Slave." In it, twentieth-century poet Harriet Wheatley presented the idea of an inner life of freedom despite chains and confinement. I never forgot that poem, and my research for *No More!* confirmed the rightness of her idea. Throughout the brutal, humiliating experience of slavery, many African Americans resisted and lived their "inner" freedom.

Their music, culture, and community nurtured them until they were free.

In *No More!* I have attempted to trace the courageous struggle waged by enslaved Africans from the time they boarded the first slave ships heading for the New World to emancipation with the ratification of the Thirteenth Amendment.

I searched for voices that would tell the story in the most immediate way possible, going back to the Black spirituals, reading slave narratives, folktales, and autobiographies, and interweaving some of these voices with my own. My descriptions of the actions and feelings of Frederick Douglass, Olaudah Equiano, John Scobell, William Still, Suzie King Taylor, Nat Turner, and Booker T. Washington come directly from auto-biographies and interviews. The "hush-harbor" meeting and the attempted mutiny were re-created from a number of first-person accounts: Vina and Aunt Peggy are composites of real people. Caroline was an actual person, but we know little about her other than her first name.

I am grateful to artist Shane W. Evans, who has interpreted these historical events and figures through his unique vision, always respecting the original sources.

I remain in awe of the courage and dignity of the enslaved African Americans. And I remain in awe of their inventive defiance and resistance under the hideous system called slavery. ▬

MY PA
WAS NEVER SLAVE

Slave?

My pa was never slave.

And those

Who thought   they made him slave,   didn't

Understand

The word.

He saw beyond the cottonfields and

Cornfields

That blinded

Their eyes;

Beyond the valleys, dark with their sins, the
        sunrise,

They

Could not conceive. This,

                        Pa knew.

                                This,   I know.

HARRIET WHEATLEY

Historians believe that in a span of 350 years, millions of Africans were sold into slavery. Millions died marching across Africa to the sea. They died on the Middle Passage, the sea route across the Atlantic Ocean to the New World. They died on slave ships from beatings, from lack of food and water, and from dysentery, smallpox, and fevers contracted in the filthy quarters below deck. The sick and the dead were thrown to the sharks.

Olaudah Equiano survived the Middle Passage, but it took him twenty years to buy back his freedom. When he was first kidnapped and enslaved, he was ten years old.

The Story of Olaudah

Olaudah sees the stranger with the pale complexion and long, scraggly hair point to him. *What does this ugly man want with me?* It has been seven months since Olaudah was kidnapped. Since then, he has been sold and resold. He has been taken to many different places and has seen many different strangers. None had faded skin like this man.

The stranger grabs Olaudah.

Olaudah struggles to free himself but cannot. He is forced to march with other young boys and men over sandy hills for what seems like hours, until they stop at the edge of the ocean. *What kind of water is this that stretches forever?* He is made to climb a steep wooden plank onto a cargo ship. *What kind of boat is this that stretches forever?* Another white man pokes his arms and chest and legs. *Where am I?* Olaudah looks around and sees men, women, and children with frightened eyes. Chains around their wrists and legs bind them together. Copper flames leap from a large hole in the floor of the boat.

No, no! Suddenly he knows where he is. In the world of evil spirits. He is going to be sacrificed. Broiled and eaten. His mother has misnamed him. He is *not* Olaudah. He is *not* fortunate. His knees collapse and he falls onto the wooden deck.

Push. Shove. Push. Shove. He is forced down a ladder to a long, dark room where black men in chains lie wedged together on wooden planks. The smell of sweat and vomit fills Olaudah's nostrils, and he gags. Amid the moans and cries, he hears his own language spoken. "What is to be done with us?" he asks. "We are going to their country to work for them" is the answer. These few words temporarily soothe him. For now, at least, he isn't going to die. ▬

From the moment they were forcibly taken from their families, Africans resisted the enslavement of their bodies and their spirits. On slave ships some Africans refused to eat. Some jumped overboard, choosing death over slavery. Mutinies happened so often that slave traders bought insurance to cover their losses in case of a slave rebellion.

The Story of Peppel

Peppel breathes in the fresh air above the deck. How good it feels to stretch without heavy chains on his legs and hands. If only he could stay up here forever. But no. "Down you go again," a sailor barks. Peppel and the other seven captives don't understand the man's words, but they know what is expected. They climb back down the ladder to the hot, stinking hold. They hurry down the passageway, fearful of being whipped if they don't move fast enough. Peppel glances over his shoulder. The sailor has disappeared from view.

Peppel stops to rub his sore hands and raw wrists, and suddenly he feels like laughing. The sailor forgot to put back his chains and leg irons! He grabs the shoulder of the man in front of him and raises his hands triumphantly. The man looks down at his own bare hands in disbelief. And so the news is passed from man to man. Silently, instantly, a plan is made.

For hours they crouch in the dark passageway, waiting for night. When they think it is time, they

retrace their steps to the ladder. Miraculously, the sailor has also forgotten to replace the iron grate that locks them in below.

They creep onto the deck. The only sound is the gentle slap of waves against the ship. A full moon casts a brilliant light on a lone sentry strutting back and forth. Peppel raises his hand in signal and two men pounce on the sentry's back. Peppel pulls at the sentry's cutlass, but it is fastened to his waist with a short piece of rope.

The sentry shouts, "Help, help!"

The rope holding the sword is so twisted that Peppel cannot pull it free.

"Help, help!" the sentry shouts again.

Now Peppel hears the clamor of running feet and the shouts of approaching crew members. He lets go of the cutlass and jumps overboard. His seven companions follow. Their arms flail as they bob up and down in the water. Between mouthfuls of salty water, Peppel cries out for someone to show him how to swim.

A rowboat is lowered from the ship. Hands stretch out to pull the drowning men into the boat. Peppel's only other choice is the bottom of the dark, cold ocean. He reaches out and puts his black hand into the white hands of his captors. ■

The largest demand for slaves came from the southern part of what would become the United States of America. Many hands were needed there to grow tobacco, rice, sugar, and cotton. Arriving in this New World, the Africans were examined and auctioned off to the highest bidders. They were always in danger of being separated from their loved ones—husbands from wives, parents from children.

William Rino sold Henry Silvers,
　　Hilo! Hilo!
Sold him to de Gorgy* trader,
　　Hilo! Hilo!
His wife she cried and children bawled,
　　Hilo! Hilo!
Sold him to de Gorgy trader,
　　Hilo! Hilo!

TRADITIONAL SONG, MELODY UNKNOWN

*possible reference to state of Georgia

In this unfamiliar land, escape seemed impossible. But resistance continued. Every day, however they could, slaves tried to gain some control over their lives. Being subtle and deceptive and invisible was crucial to that resistance.

Working under the whip

from sunrise to sunset,

they misplaced hoes,

planted less rice,

picked less cotton,

poked holes in tobacco netting,

broke saws and axes and shovels,

busted fences and

burned crops.

They stole

the master's chickens and his pigs

and his corn and his flour

because they were starving.

They lied to protect themselves.

They forged passes

to visit wives and husbands and

   children

sold or transferred to nearby

   plantations or cities.

At night in the slave quarters,

they spoke their African names

and told their children of the

cerulean blue sky in their village

and the rich dark soil

where cotton plants shot up wild

and a yam grew so big it fed a family.

DOREEN RAPPAPORT

Song and story had been essential parts of life in Africa, and so it was here. As the newly enslaved Africans learned a new language, they created new songs to describe their new lives. They counted up the wrongs inflicted on them and vented their outrage.

We raise de wheat,

Dey gib us de corn;

We bake de bread,

Dey gib us de crust;

We sift de meal,

Dey gib us de husk;

We peel de meat,

Dey gib us de skin,

And dat's de way,

Dey take us in;

Dey skim de pot,

Dey gib us de likker*,

And say dat's good enough
  for nigger.

TRADITIONAL SONG, MELODY UNKNOWN

*reference to liquor, meaning the liquid in
 which meat has been boiled.

Elders told stories to teach the young how to survive in this harsh world. They retold African trickster tales of how the rabbit outwitted the wily fox, or how the tiny mouse tricked the cat. New stories, about "Old Marsa" and John, the slave trickster, were born. Knowing that the weak sometimes triumph over the strong made the children feel more hopeful and confident.

The Story of Vina

Mama hugs Vina. After sixteen hours of bending over in the rice fields, it feels good to be in Mama's arms, sitting on the warm earth.

An elder named Aunt Peggy begins. "Well, there was that time when John stole a pig from Old Marsa. . . ." Oh, how Vina loves the stories about John, the slave trickster. "John was on his way home with the pig and his Old Marsa seen him."

Aunt Peggy rapidly slaps the side of her leg, and Vina can hear John running on the road. Aunt Peggy gives out a series of oinks and squeals, and Vina can feel the pig squirming to get free from John's grip.

"After John got home, he looked out and seen his Old Marsa coming down to the house." More footsteps. "So John put this pig in a cradle they used to rock babies in them days, and he covered him up. When Old Marsa come in, John was sitting there rocking the cradle." Aunt Peggy sways in rhythm with the creaking cradle.

"Old Marsa says, 'What's the matter with the baby, John?' "

Creak, creak.

" 'The baby got the measles,' answered John."

Creak, Creak.

" 'I want to see him,' Old Marsa says."

The creaking stops.

" 'Well you can't,' cries John. 'The doctor said if you uncover him the measles will go back in on him and kill him.'

"So Old Marsa says, 'It doesn't matter. I want to see him, John.'

"As Old Marsa reached down to uncover the pig, John jumped up and shouted, 'If that baby is turned to a pig now, don't blame me!' "

Before the laughter has time to evaporate into the warm night air, Aunt Peggy starts another story. Then another. And so it goes until Vina falls asleep in Mama's arms. ▪

In the New World, slave owners forced the first Africans to practice their religion. Defiantly, the Africans mixed their own rituals with this imposed Christianity. Deep in the woods, they created secret places of worship. In these "hush harbors," they retold Old Testament stories of how God delivered the Hebrews, and created their own songs to comfort and empower themselves. Most slave owners never knew that Christianity had become quiet resistance.

The Story of Adeline

Away from the master's house. Away from the slave cabins. Away from the white patrols guarding the plantation, Adeline follows the bent boughs on the trees and runs with joy into the woods.

Wet quilts and rags hang on trees to make the shape of a small room and to keep sound from traveling. Adeline pushes aside a quilt and joins a circle of people kneeling. On the ground are many wash pots filled with water to further muffle sound. The slave preacher leans over a pot and begins. "And so King Darius punished the young boy. . . ."

The preacher's body trembles as he recounts how Daniel was thrown into a den of lions. He stretches his arms over his head as if to pull Heaven down to Earth. Wide-eyed, he explains how God tamed the hungry lions and rescued Daniel.

"Didn't my Lord deliver Daniel, deliver Daniel, deliver Daniel. . . ."

Adeline sings with the others. Their

voices quaver as they slide off the melody. Bodies sway, knees shake. Feet stamp one rhythm, hands clap another. Some people groan. Others moan. A woman next to Adeline raises her head and shouts. Adeline fears the patrollers will hear, and she gently pushes the woman's head back down toward the wash pot.

All is joy and power and hope as Adeline sings about how God delivered the Hebrews to freedom. She knows her people are the chosen people too. As the Hebrews were imprisoned in Egypt, her people are imprisoned now. But God will surely lead them to freedom. ▪

Didn't My Lord Deliver Daniel?

Lively (with spirit)

Did - n't my Lord de - liv - er Dan - iel,___ de - liv - er

Dan - iel,___ de - liv - er Dan - iel,___ Did - n't my Lord de - liv - er

Dan - iel,_____ And why not - a ev - e - ry man? Did - n't

man. He de - liv - ered Dan - iel from the li - on's den,

Jo - nah from the bel - ly of the whale, And the He - brew chil - dren from the

fi - er - y fur - nace, And why not ev - er - y man.

Some slaves were openly rebellious. They defied overseers and owners with words and fists and teeth and feet. Such slaves were usually sold. The owner of Frederick August Washington Bailey came up with his own solution to "tame" his most rebellious slave. He rented sixteen-year-old Frederick to a poor tenant farmer known as a "nigger-breaker."

The Story of Frederick

Every muscle in Frederick's body aches. He leans on the pitchfork and stretches his tired neck. For the last six months, Edward Covey has worked him sixteen hours a day, six days a week, in rain, hail, and broiling sun. Frederick's back is scarred from Covey's whippings. Covey has finally broken his spirit and body. Now he dreams of suicide, not freedom.

Frederick pitches a last forkful of hay down from the loft. There is more than enough now to feed the horses. As he climbs down the ladder, he feels a rope tighten around his right leg. Even without turning around, he knows it is Covey, come to torment him again. He jerks away and falls off the ladder into the dirt. Covey leans over him and clucks his tongue in triumph. Frederick looks up at Covey's sneering mouth and vicious eyes, and suddenly fury sweeps over him. Maybe he will be whipped for it. Maybe he will be hanged for it. But he's not going to let Covey beat him anymore. He springs up and seizes Covey by the throat. He

presses so hard that he pierces the skin, and blood rushes out. He kicks Covey in the ribs.

"Do you mean to persist in your resistance?" Covey shouts.

"I mean to resist, come what might. I will not let you use me like a brute any longer."

Covey grabs Frederick's arms to drag him across the barn floor. Frederick wrenches free and flings Covey to the ground.

For nearly two hours they roll in the dirt. With every punch, Frederick feels more powerful. When the fight is over, he is still a slave, but refusing to be whipped has made him feel more than half free. ▪

Covey never laid a hand on Frederick again. Four years later, Frederick escaped to the North, and shed his slave name. As Frederick Douglass, he became one of the country's most important abolitionists. In his autobiography he wrote that by fighting Covey he regained his dignity and determination to be free.

Before the Civil War ended, slave resistance erupted into more than two hundred armed uprisings. In August 1831, Nat Turner led seventy slaves in a two-day armed rebellion in Virginia. Fifty-seven whites were murdered. Nat Turner was tried and hanged, along with twenty others. Before Turner died, he explained where he had gotten the idea to lead the uprising:

> *When I was three or four years old, I was telling my playmates something that had happened before I was born. People said I would surely be a prophet. One day, when a book was shown to me, I began spelling the names of different objects. Whenever I was able to look at a book, I would find many things that my fertile imagination had depicted to me before.*
>
> *As I was praying one day at my plow, a spirit that spoke to the Prophets in former days said to me, "Seek ye the kingdom of Heaven and all things shall be added unto you." I felt that I was ordained for some great purpose in the hands of the Almighty. Several years later, I heard a loud noise in the heavens, and the spirit instantly appeared. It said that by a sign, an eclipse of the sun, Heaven would make known to me when I should arise and slay my enemies with their own weapons.*

Nat Turner's rebellion horrified white Southerners. They were stunned to realize that blacks were willing to kill and die for freedom. They became convinced that reading and writing were dangerous tools. It was Nat Turner's reading of the Bible that convinced him that God had chosen him to lead his people out of slavery. Fearing more rebellions, Southern lawmakers passed harsher slave codes. It became illegal to teach blacks to read or write.

But the fire to learn was not easily put out. Slaves taught themselves, secretly decoding the letters in their owners' books and in the Bible. Black children begged and coaxed white playmates to teach them.

Like other African Americans, Suzie King Taylor's grandmother, Dolly Reed, risked jail and beatings to have her loved ones educated at a secret school run by a free black woman.

The Story of Suzie King Taylor

The paper crinkles as Grandma wraps the package to conceal its contents. She gives the precious parcel to Suzie and her younger brother, then shoos them out the door.

Clippety-clop, clippety-clop. The streets of Savannah, Georgia, are crowded with horse-drawn carriages. Suzie longs to look at the horses and their shiny manes, but she doesn't dare. Grandma has taught her never to stare at white people or their property. On the sidewalk a white man brushes past her.

She jumps down into the street to get out of his way.

At the corner, Suzie and her brother stop. They peer about to be sure that no white people can see them. Suzie's eyes signal her brother. *Go, go!* Grandma has warned them never to enter Mrs. Woodhouse's together.

Suzie watches her brother walk down the street. Through the gate. Into the yard. Into the kitchen. She looks around again. No one is watching. She hurries down the street. Mrs. Woodhouse's kitchen is warm and welcoming. Suzie takes her place on the floor, joining thirty other black children. The paper crinkles as she unwraps the package. Out come two books. One for Suzie, one for her brother. They place their books on their laps and look up, anxious for Mrs. Woodhouse to begin the reading lesson. ▬

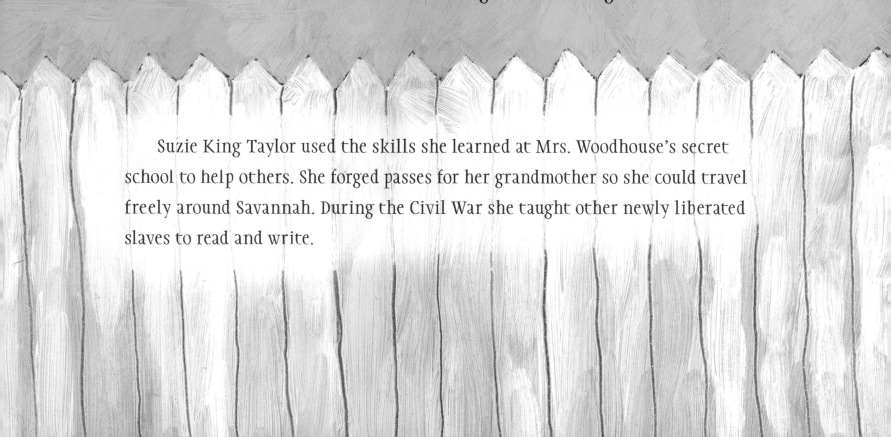

Suzie King Taylor used the skills she learned at Mrs. Woodhouse's secret school to help others. She forged passes for her grandmother so she could travel freely around Savannah. During the Civil War she taught other newly liberated slaves to read and write.

Slaves ran away all the time. For a day. A week. A month. Or forever. Moses Grandy's mother took her children to the woods and hid them there until her owner promised never to sell them. John Farmer's slaves were resigned to his drunken rages, but when he threatened to move west and separate them from their families, they ran away. When John Goings's owner died, John simply saddled up one of Goings's horses and rode off.

Some runaways found jobs in cities and passed as free blacks. Others went to live with the Cherokee and Seminole peoples. Runaways hid in mountains, forests, and remote, impenetrable areas like the Great Dismal Swamp in Virginia, or Elliott's Cut in South Carolina, or the Everglades in Florida. Some runaways returned when their owners gave in to their demands, or when they ran out of food or places to hide.

The dream was to get to "the Promised Land"—the Northern states, or Canada, or Mexico. It was a daring and reckless idea, for most slaves knew little of the world beyond the plantations and towns and cities of the South.

Like many black spirituals, "Steal Away to Jesus" is both a lament and a protest. In it, God is calling his people to freedom. Jesus will be at their side, for he suffered and understands their pain.

Steal Away to Jesus

Very slowly, with expression

Steal a-way, steal a-way, steal a-way to Je - sus!

Fine

Steal a-way, steal a-way home, I ain't got long to stay here.

1. My Lord ____ calls me, He calls me by the thun - der; The
2. Green trees are bend - ing, poor sin - ner stands a - trem-bling; The
3. Tomb-stones are burst-ing, poor sin - ner stands a - trem-bling; The
4. My Lord ____ calls me, he calls me by the light - ning; The

D.C.

trum-pet sounds with in - a my soul, I ain't got long to stay here.

Desperate and determined to be free, black men, women, and children followed the constellation they called the Drinking Gourd north. Using the Big Dipper and the North Star as their compass, they crossed swamps and rivers and mountains, not knowing what was on the other side. It is believed that as many as 100,000 succeeded in escaping. Historical records tell of a woman named Caroline who escaped with her children from Kentucky to Indiana.

The Story of Caroline
—

Swamp slime soaks the bottom of Caroline's skirt. She pays it no mind. Bullfrogs croak and crickets chirp. She does not listen to their songs. The night sky glitters with points of light. Caroline's eyes are fixed only on the North Star, her compass to freedom. She carries the youngest of her children and leads the others through the mire.

One mile. Two miles. Mud clings to their clothes and weighs them down. Caroline can no longer see her compass. A thick canopy of leaves blocks the sky. One child falls. Caroline scoops him out of the mud. "Keep going, keep going," she urges. Finally they reach the other side of the swamp, and they see the sky again.

The North Star and the Drinking Gourd shine brightly. Caroline's hope lifts her up. ▬

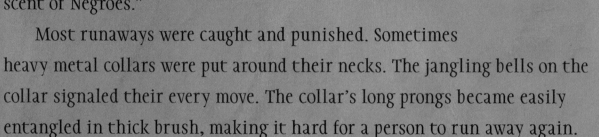

Slaveholders pursued their "property." Wherever there were walls or posts, they plastered handbills offering rewards for runaways. Bounty hunters tracked them, using dogs supposedly trained to "pick up the scent of Negroes."

Most runaways were caught and punished. Sometimes heavy metal collars were put around their necks. The jangling bells on the collar signaled their every move. The collar's long prongs became easily entangled in thick brush, making it hard for a person to run away again.

Captured. Imprisoned. Beaten to near death. Branded. Handcuffed to logs. Forbidden to visit loved ones. Auctioned off. They plotted their next escape.

Run, nigger, run, patroller'll ketch ya,
Hit ya thirty-nine and swear he didn't tech ya.

TRADITIONAL SONG, MELODY UNKNOWN

By 1840 there were over a thousand groups of people in the North and Midwest working to abolish slavery. Black and white men and women lectured against slavery. Most times they were booed off the stage or tarred and feathered or shot at. They published books and newspapers that were banned in the South. Some abolitionists joined the Underground Railroad, a secret network of helpers and routes north. "Stationmasters" hid runaways in attics, barns, cellars, and secret rooms. "Conductors" led them on foot, by horseback, by canoe, and in wagons with secret compartments. Helpers risked jail, fines, and death.

"Gospel Train" is about religious faith, but it is also about the Underground Railroad.

Gospel Train

Allegro

Get on board, lit-tle chil-dren, Get on board, lit-tle chil-dren, Get on

board, lit-tle chil-dren, There's room for ma-ny a more. The

gos-pel train's a-com-in', I hear it just at hand. I hear the car wheels mov-in', An'

rumb-lin' thro the land. Get on board, lit-tle chil-dren, Get on board, lit-tle chil-dren, Get on

board, lit-tle chil-dren, There's room for ma-ny a more. The fare is cheap, an' all can go, The

rich an' poor are there. No sec-ond class a-board this train, No

diff'-rence in the fare. Get on board, lit-tle chil-dren, Get on board, lit-tle chil-dren, get on

board, lit-tle chil-dren, There's room for man-y a more.

William Still was born a free black, but his parents had been born slaves. His father had bought his freedom. His mother escaped, was captured, and fled a second time successfully.

William headed a "vigilance" committee of white and black abolitionists in Philadelphia, Pennsylvania. Its members gave runaways shelter, food, clothing, money, and transportation farther north. William interviewed every runaway who came through the city. He recorded their escapes so that their courage and ingenuity would become part of American history:

February 26, 1854: *John Mercer, William H. Gilliam, and John Clayton came by steamer in a space not far from the boiler, where the heat and coal dust were almost intolerable. The colored steward on the boat could point to no other place for concealment but this. It admitted of no other posture than lying flat down, wholly shut out from the light, and nearly from the air.*

May 31, 1856: *Charlotte Giles and Harriet Eglin escaped from Baltimore by dressing in mourning with heavy black veils. While seated in the railroad car before leaving Baltimore, who should enter but Charlotte's master. In a very excited manner, he hurriedly approached Charlotte and Harriet, who pretended to be weeping. Peeping under their veils, he exclaimed, "What is your name?"*

"Mary, sir," sobbed Charlotte.

"What is your name?" he asked Harriet.

"Lizzie, sir," was the faint reply.

The gentleman rushed on through the cars as if moved by steam, looking for his property. Not finding it, and to the delight of Charlotte and Harriet, he soon disappeared.

One blistering hot August day, William Still interviewed a man named Peter Freedman. Peter had bought his freedom after forty-eight years and was now looking to find his parents. "What were your parents' names?" William asked. "Your older brother's name? Your owner?" Question after question. Peter's answers startled William. Peter Freedman was his brother. ▬

Harriet Tubman, the most beloved conductor on the Underground Railroad, was a runaway slave. A price of $40,000 was put on her head, but that did not stop her from returning to the South. Nineteen times she risked death to lead others to freedom.

"Go Down Moses" tells of the flight of the Jews from slavery in Egypt to freedom in Palestine. The song is in code. "Egypt Land" means the South. "Pharaoh" refers to Southern slaveholders. "Moses" is Harriet Tubman.

Go Down Moses

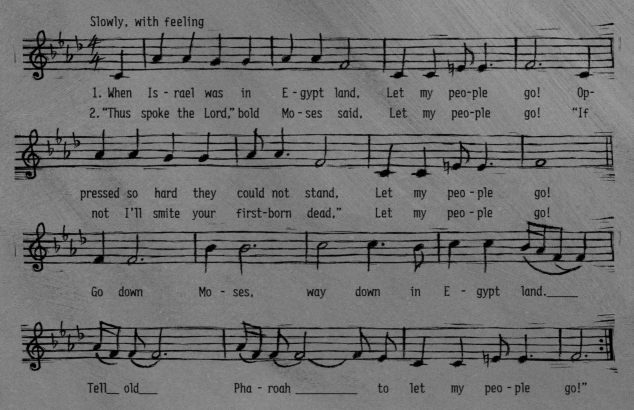

Slowly, with feeling

1. When Is - rael was in E - gypt land, Let my peo - ple go! Op-
2. "Thus spoke the Lord," bold Mo - ses said, Let my peo - ple go! "If

pressed so hard they could not stand, Let my peo - ple go!
not I'll smite your first-born dead," Let my peo - ple go!

Go down Mo - ses, way down in E - gypt land.____

Tell__ old__ Pha - roah _____ to let my peo - ple go!"

Slave uprisings. Abolitionists. The Underground Railroad. White Southerners became angrier and angrier, fearing that their way of life might end.

Slavery became the major campaign issue in the American presidential election of 1860. The newly formed Republican Party did not want slavery extended into the western territories. Shortly after Republican Abraham Lincoln won the presidential election, South Carolina, Florida, Alabama, Georgia, Louisiana, Mississippi, and Texas seceded from the union. Five months later the Civil War began.

Free blacks and slaves had fought with distinction in the American Revolution and the War of 1812. They were eager to fight with the Union now. Frederick Douglass urged President Lincoln to enlist free blacks. Douglass was shocked and angered when Lincoln rejected the idea. The President feared that the border states would leave the Union if blacks were allowed to fight. Most white Northerners weren't eager to fight alongside black men, whom they considered inferior. In fact, most Northern soldiers were not fighting to end slavery. They were fighting to bring the Southern states back into the Union.

Their enlistment refused, free blacks formed their own militia units. Runaways worked as road builders, camp attendants, cooks, scouts, guides, and spies. Harriet Tubman spied behind Confederate lines. Suzie King Taylor nursed the wounded in the Union Army.

John Scobell was a runaway slave and was uniquely qualified to be a spy. He knew the Southern landscape, the nightly routes of the patrollers, and the sites of Confederate camps. He teamed up with Timothy Webster and solved many a problem that stumped his white partner.

The Story of John Scobell

John Scobell hurries across the hotel lobby and sits down next to Timothy Webster. He leans over and whispers, "I've found an intelligent and loyal colored man who'll deliver the documents."

"How can we be sure he won't betray us?" Webster doesn't know anyone he can trust in the Confederate town of Leonardsville, Virginia.

A quick smile appears on Scobell's face. "He won't," he says confidently.

Webster follows Scobell to a deserted street on the outskirts of town. Scobell stops at a brick building with wooden boards nailed over the windows. He knocks three times on the door. It swings open. The two men step into darkness. Scobell gives a single shrill whistle.

"Who comes?" a deep voice calls out.

"Friends of Uncle Abe," Scobell answers.

"What do you desire?"

"Light and loyalty!" answers Scobell.

An overhead door drops open. A rope ladder is lowered. The ladder swings back and forth as

Scobell and Webster climb. At the top they find themselves in a dim loft.

Webster counts at least forty black men. Most are young. All are standing but one. That man sits on a packing crate near a barrel draped with an American flag. He welcomes them to this meeting of the Leonardsville, Virginia, Lodge of the Loyal League. He does not offer his name or the names of the other men. Webster and John know not to ask. Secrecy is a matter of life and death for all Union sympathizers in the South, especially Negroes.

Scobell quickly explains their problem. He has stolen important Confederate documents that must be delivered swiftly to Washington, D.C.

"It will be no trouble for me to find my way there," says a man of about thirty-five years.

And Webster believes him. Scobell has led him to the right people. Any of the men in the room could do this job better than he or Scobell. They know their way through the forests and swamps. They know where and how to cross the rivers.

Assured and grateful, Timothy Webster accepts the offer. John Scobell sews the documents into the lining of the man's coat and whispers the name of the person to see. Two days later the documents arrive in the capital of the Union. ▬

On January 1, 1863, President Lincoln signed the Emancipation Proclamation. It freed all slaves in the Confederacy and in territories in rebellion. Within a month black regiments were formed.

On May 28, 1863, trumpets blared and flags and banners waved as twenty thousand Bostonians cheered the Fifty-fourth Regiment of Massachusetts Volunteers of African Descent marching off to battle. Frederick Douglass's son Lewis marched with them.

Close to 179,000 African-American men fought for the Union. Of those, 93,000 had been born slaves. Blacks served in 166 segregated regiments in the infantry, heavy artillery, light artillery, and cavalry. They sailed on Union navy ships. They fought on battlefields in Virginia, Arkansas, Mississippi, Tennessee, and South Carolina. Although black Americans were only one percent of the population of the United States, they made up twelve percent of Union forces.

Many Thousand Gone

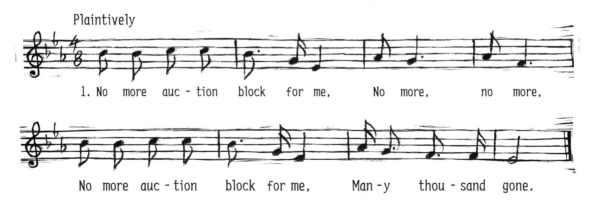

Plaintively

1. No more auc - tion block for me, No more, no more,

No more auc - tion block for me, Man - y thou - sand gone.

2. No more peck of corn for me, etc.

3. No more driver's lash for me, etc.

4. No more pint of salt for me, etc.

5. No more hundred lash for me, etc.

6. No more mistress' call for me, etc.

The Civil War ended on April 9, 1865, when Confederate general Robert E. Lee formally surrendered to Union general Ulysses S. Grant. Thirty-eight thousand African-American men had died to save the Union and to end slavery. President Lincoln summed up their impact simply: "Without the military help of black freed men, the war against the South could not have been won."

The Story of Booker T. Washington

Standing on the veranda of the Big House, nine-year-old Booker snuggles into the crook of his mother's arm. A white man in a blue uniform starts to talk. Booker does not understand all his big words but he senses their importance. When the man finishes speaking, his words are greeted with silence and awe. Then Booker's mother hugs him so tight he can hardly breathe. Tears stream down her face as she kisses him and his sister and brother. "I prayed many times for this day," she says. "But I never believed I would live to see it." Then Booker knows. They are free! Every last one of the slaves on James Burroughs's plantation. Free! ▬

On December 18, 1865, the Thirteenth Amendment to the Constitution, abolishing slavery in all states and territories, became the law of the reunited land. Black men, women, and children set out to meet their next challenge — *freedom.*

IMPORTANT DATES

1619 The first twenty African settlers arrive in Jamestown, Virginia, as indentured servants.

1641 Slavery becomes legal in Massachusetts. Between 1650 and 1750 other colonies follow: Connecticut in 1650; Virginia in 1661; Maryland, New York, and New Jersey in 1664; South Carolina in 1682; Rhode Island and Pennsylvania in 1700; North Carolina in 1715; and Georgia in 1750.

1663 White and indentured servants band together in the first recorded slave conspiracy, in Gloucester, Virginia. They are captured.

1755 Olaudah Equiano is shipped off to the New World as a slave.

1776 The Declaration of Independence, which states that "all men are created equal," is approved. The final draft omits Thomas Jefferson's attack on the King of England for allowing the slave trade.

1777–1804 Northern states gradually abolish slavery. By 1804, all states north of Delaware have outlawed slavery.

1787 Congress adopts the Constitution. The "Three-fifths Compromise" allows the Southern states to count three-fifths of their slave population to determine representation in the House of Representatives. The Northwest Ordinance, passed in the same year, bars slavery in the Northwest Territories.

1793 The Fugitive Slave Act makes it a crime to help escaped slaves or to interfere in their arrest. It denies slaves a trial by jury or the right to testify on their own behalf. Whites helping fugitives are subject to fines and imprisonment.

1808 Federal law ends the importing of slaves to the United States.

1820 The Missouri Compromise admits Missouri to the Union as a slave state and admits Maine as a free state. Slavery is prohibited north of 36° 30' latitude.

1831 Nat Turner leads a rebellion of seventy slaves in Virginia.

1834 Frederick Douglass fights with Edward Covey.

1850 The Compromise of 1850 admits California to the Union as a free state but leaves open the question of slavery in the Utah and New Mexico territories.

1851 Harriet Tubman takes her first trip back to the South to lead nine African Americans to freedom.

1856 Suzie King Taylor begins attending Mrs. Woodhouse's secret school.

1857 In the case of *Scott v. Sanford*, the U.S. Supreme Court rules that blacks, whether free or enslaved, are not U.S. citizens.

1860 Abraham Lincoln is elected president. Within five months, seven Southern states secede from the Union and form the Confederacy.

1861 On April 21, Confederate troops fire on Fort Sumter, and the Civil War begins.

1863 John Scobell becomes a spy for the Union during the Civil War.

1863 The Emancipation Proclamation is signed on January 1, ending slavery in the Confederate states.

1864 Booker T. Washington learns he is free.

1865 The Civil War ends, April 9. The Thirteenth Amendment to the Constitution is enacted on December 18, outlawing slavery in the United States.

1872 William Still's book, *The Underground Railroad*, is published.

Acknowledgments and Sources

I thank the superb reference librarians at the Schomburg Center for Black Culture; Daisy Rosenblum for her research skills and insight; Eli Zaretsky, professor of history at the New School University, for critiquing the manuscript in its many incarnations; Dorothy Carter, Professor Emerita of Children's Literature, Bank Street College of Education, for critiquing the manuscript; and Bob Rosegarten for joining this adventure with humor and intelligence. I am especially grateful to Mary Lee Donovan for her editorial expertise and passion for this material.

I found the real-life accounts in newspaper articles, diaries, journals, first-person accounts, and books. I compared sources to create the most accurate picture. "Baby in the Crib" is reprinted with the permission of Gloria Dorson, F.O.B. Richard Dorson Trust.

Folktales and spirituals were passed orally from generation to generation. Interested performers, folklorists, and musicologists recorded African Americans singing this unique body of literature and transcribed what they heard. There are many versions of these songs and tales because improvisation was and is a large part of the black musical experience.

The language spoken by the enslaved Africans was then a transitional language between their native languages and English. It was constantly changing, but too often the transcribers did not pick up these subtleties. In some of the poems and songs in this book, I kept the words as transcribed because they effectively transmit the rhythm and intense feelings. In other cases, I chose words and spellings that would be most accessible to children.

While every effort has been made to obtain permission to reprint copyright material, there may be cases where I have been unable to trace a copyright holder. Despite extensive research, I was not able to find Harriet Wheatley. The publisher will be happy to correct any omission in future printings.

—

Selected books used in research:

Douglass, Frederick. *My Bondage and My Freedom*, with an introduction by Dr. James M'Cune Smith. New York: Auburn, Miller, Orton & Mulligan, ca. 1855.

Dow, George Francis. *Slave Ships and Slaving*. New York: Dover Publications, 1970 (reprint).

Equiano, Olaudah. *Equiano's travels; the interesting narrative of the life of Olaudah Equiano or Gustavus Vassa, the African*. Abridged and edited by Paul Edwards. New York: Praeger, 1967.

Franklin, John Hope, and Loren Schweninger. *Runaway Slaves: Rebels on the Plantation*. New York and Oxford: Oxford University Press, 1999.

Levine, Laurence. *Black Culture and Black Consciousness*. New York and London: Oxford University Press, 1977.

Smith, E. L. "Baby in the Crib." In *Negro Folktales in Michigan*, by Richard Mercer Dorson. Cambridge: Harvard University Press, 1956.

Still, William. *The Underground Railroad*. Philadelphia: Porter and Coates, 1872.

Taylor, Suzie King. *Reminiscences of my life in camp with the 33rd United States colored troops, late 1st S. C. volunteers.* Boston: The Author, 1902.

——

To learn more about the people mentioned in this book, you can read:

Adler, David. *A Picture Book of Frederick Douglass.* Illustrated by Samuel Byrd. New York: Holiday House, 1997.

Bentley, Judith. *Dear Friend: Thomas Garrett and William Still, Collaborators on the Underground Railroad.* New York: New American Library, 1997.

Bial, Raymond. *The Underground Railroad.* Boston: Houghton Mifflin, 1995.

Bisson, Terry. *Nat Turner.* Broomall, PA: Chelsea House, 1991.

Equiano, Olaudah. *The Slave Who Bought His Freedom: Equiano's Story,* adapted by Karen Kennedy. New York: Dutton, 1971.

Haskins, James. *Black, Blue and Gray: African Americans in the Civil War.* New York: Simon and Schuster, 1998.

——. *Get On Board: The Story of the Underground Railroad.* New York: Scholastic, 1993.

Jordan, Denise. *Suzie King Taylor: Destined to Be Free.* East Orange, NJ: Just Us Books, 1996.

Lester, Julius. *From Slave Ship to Freedom Road.* Illustrated by Rod Brown. New York: Dial Books for Young Readers, 1998.

Levine, Ellen. *If You Traveled on the Underground Railroad.* New York: Scholastic, 1988.

Rappaport, Doreen. *Escape from Slavery.* New York: Harper Trophy, 1998.

——. *Freedom River.* New York: Hyperion, 2000.

Ringgold, Faith. *Aunt Harriet's Underground Railroad in the Sky.* New York: Dial Books for Young Readers, 1995.

A search of the Web using the words Frederick Douglass, Underground Railroad, Underground Railroad Museum, Harriet Tubman, and Slavery leads to hundreds of sites and links in the United States.

Index

abolitionists, 42, 44–45
abolition of slavery, 54–57
Adeline, 24–27
auctions of slaves, 18–19

Bailey, Frederick August
  Washington, 28–31
black regiments, 52–54
bounty hunters, 40
Burroughs, James, 54

Caroline, 38–39
Cherokees, 36
Christianity, 24, 37
Civil War, 35, 47–54, 57
Clayton, John, 44
coded messages, 46
Compromise of 1850, 57
Confederacy, 47, 48, 50, 52, 54, 57
Constitution, 55, 56, 57
Covey, Edward, 29–31, 57

Declaration of Independence, 56
"Didn't My Lord Deliver Daniel?", 27
Douglass, Frederick, 28–31, 47, 52, 57
Douglass, Lewis, 52
Drinking Gourd (Big Dipper), 38

Eglin, Harriet, 44
Elliott's Cut, 36
Emancipation Proclamation, 52, 57
Equiano, Olaudah, 10, 12–13, 56
Everglades, 36

Farmer, John, 36
Fifty-fourth Regiment, 52, 54
free blacks, 34, 36, 44, 47, 52, 54
Freedman, Peter, 45
fugitives. See runaways
Fugitive Slave Act, 56–57

Giles, Charlotte, 44
Gilliam, William H., 44
"Go Down Moses," 46–47
Goings, John, 36
"Gospel Train," 43
Grandy, Moses, 36
Grant, Ulysses S., 54
Great Dismal Swamp, 36

House of Representatives, 56
"hush harbors," 24

Jefferson, Thomas, 56
Jews, 46

Lee, Robert E., 54
Lincoln, Abraham, 47, 52, 54, 57
Lodge of the Loyal League, 50

"Many Thousand Gone," 52
Massachusetts Volunteers of
  African Descent, 52
Mercer, John, 44
metal collars, 40–41
Middle Passage, 10
militia units, 47
Missouri Compromise, 57
Moses, 46
Mrs. Woodhouse's secret
  school, 34–35, 57
"My Pa Was Never Slave," 9

Nat Turner's rebellion, 32–33, 57
Northwest Ordinance, 56

Peppel, 14–17
presidential election (1860), 47, 57

reading, 32, 34–35
Reed, Dolly, 34
religion, 24–27, 37, 43, 46
Republican Party, 47
runaways, 36–50
"Run, nigger, run," 40

Scobell, John, 48–51, 57
Scott v. Sanford, 57
secession, 47, 57
secret schools, 32, 34–35, 57
secret worship, 24–27
Seminoles, 36
slave trade, 10–17, 56, 57
songs, 21, 24, 40
spying, 47, 48–50, 57
stationmasters, 42
"Steal Away to Jesus," 37
Still, William, 44–45, 57
storytelling, 22–23
Supreme Court, 57

Taylor, Suzie King, 34–35, 47, 57
Thirteenth Amendment, 55, 57
"Three-fifths Compromise," 56
trickster tales, 22–23
Tubman, Harriet, 46–47, 57
Turner, Nat, 32, 57

Underground Railroad, 42–43, 46, 47, 57
Union Army, 47, 52–54

vigilance committees, 44–45
Vina, 22–23

Washington, Booker T., 54, 57
Webster, Timothy, 48–51
"We raise de wheat," 21
Wheatley, Harriet, 9
"William Rino sold Henry Silvers," 18
"Working under the whip," 20
writing, 32, 34–35

DOREEN RAPPAPORT is the author of many award-winning books for young readers. About creating this book, she says, "Writing a book educates the writer. The inventive defiance, humanity, and resistance forged by African Americans under the horrors of slavery reinforced for me the power of individual dignity and community." Doreen Rappaport divides her time between New York City and a rural village in upstate New York.

SHANE W. EVANS is the illustrator of several children's books. About working on this book, he says that the challenge was to share "the reality and darkness of slavery through painting. It is my goal," he explains, "to paint beautiful images, yet the subjects I depict are not always beautiful." Shane W. Evans lives in Missouri.